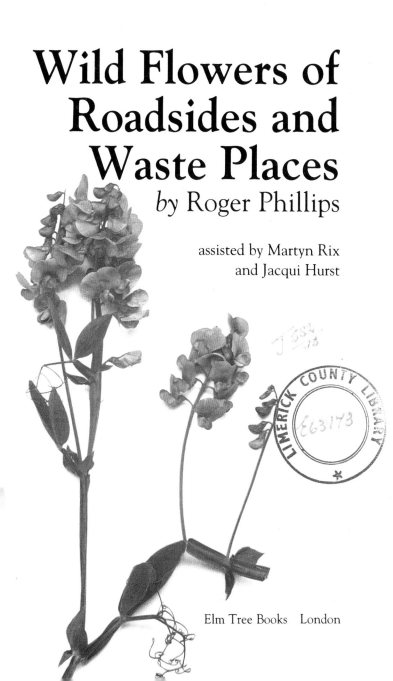

Wild Flowers of Roadsides and Waste Places

by Roger Phillips

assisted by Martyn Rix
and Jacqui Hurst

Elm Tree Books   London

INTRODUCTION

We have aimed to photogaph and describe 95 of the most conspicuous roadside plants found in the British Isles and northern Europe.

How to use this book

The flowers are arranged roughly in order of flowering, from spring to autumn. One photograph shows the most important parts of the plant, laid out so that details can be seen easily and clearly. The other shows the plant growing and gives some idea of its habitat, height, bushiness and stiffness. Sometimes, two closely related or similar species are shown together, and the distinctions between them are mentioned in the text.

What is a roadside plant?

Most of the plants in this book are conspicuous along grassy road verges, on motorway banks, railway embankments, or in other grassy waste places. In *Weeds* we concentrated on plants which preferred bare soil – they tend to be annuals and come up the first year after a new road is built, but cannot compete in a sward of coarse grass. The plants shown here are mainly perennials or really tough annuals, well able to survive competition and periodic mowing. Many, such as Goats Rue (page 78), are old herbaceous border plants; others, such as Soapwort (page 106), were formerly grown in herb gardens for use as soap, but are now exclusively roadside plants. Some, like Chicory (page 110) have probably escaped from vegetable plots, or like Lucerne (page 76) from agriculture.

Many native wild flowers have found the roadside habitat especially favourable. Hemlock (page 48), once found usually by streams, is now very common along motorways near London, and the similar but shorter

Naturalized lupins

Cow Parsley (page 12), naturally a plant of wood edges, grows happily in the open along miles of country road.

Often roadsides or ditches shelter the last remnant of the native vegetation now destroyed by intensive agriculture, the ploughing and re-seeding of pastures, and the spraying of field edges. Their maintenance and preservation is thus very important, and as it were, held in trust by the local authority concerned. Weedkillers, especially those which kill wild flowers (alias 'broad-leaved weeds') and leave grass, should not be tolerated on any account. Ideally the roadsides, or at least those patches which harbour a good range of wild species, should be mowed as late as possible in the season, so that some of the wild flowers have time to seed, and the cut grass cleared away after it has dried, so that more delicate flowers are not smothered. New roadsides should be planted with clover or a local wild flower mixture, not with a sward-forming grass which prevents seedlings of wild flowers becoming established. Where conditions are suitable, new roadsides are soon colonized by wild flowers, such as spotted orchids (page 52), cowslips or primroses (pages 8 and 9). Unless the subsoil is unstable clay, there is usually no need to replace topsoil; most wild flowers can better colonize infertile soils.

We have included here the most common of these native wild flowers, but more will be found in *Woodland Wild Flowers* (1986), and the forthcoming *Chalk and Limestone Wild Flowers*, *Heathland Wild Flowers* and *Water and Waterside Wild Flowers*.

Glossary

anther	part of flower holding pollen
bract	a modified leaf beneath a flower head, or at the base of the flower stem
calyx	outer, usually green, parts of flower
cleistogamous	specialized, usually very small flowers which set seed without opening
corymb	flat-topped head of flowers
cyme	head of flowers in which new flowers are formed in the axils of the older flowers
glabrous	smooth
involucral	around a head of flowers, of a leaf or bract
ligule	a thin piece of tissue at the junction of the leaf of a grass and the sheath
panicle	a branched inflorescence, often of a grass
pinnate	with leaflets on either side of a central stem
raceme	elongated head of flowers, opening in succession from the base
rhizome	an underground, usually creeping, stem
stipule	appendage on the stalk of a leaf
tubercle	small, warty growth
umbel/ umbellifer	many stems arising from same point, forming flat topped head of flowers

Lady's Smock

Lady's Smock or Cuckoo Flower

Cardamine pratensis (Cabbage family) is a common feature of roadside ditches and damp banks where, especially on heavy soils, it may produce beautiful drifts of pale mauve flowers. It is common throughout the British Isles, flowering from early April to June in the north. It is also found in Europe, northern Asia and North America.

Only rarely are the flowers pure white; then it resembles the rarer **Large Bittercress**, *Cardamine amara*, a flower of streams and river banks, which has smaller flowers only 12 mm in diameter, and dark purple, not yellow, stamens. Lady's Smock is very variable in other features such as height, from 15 to 60 cm, leaf shape and chromosome number, and distinct forms can cover large areas, spreading by means of stolons. A double-flowered form is known in gardens.

Cardamine pratensis

Winter Cress

Wintercress or Yellow Rocket

Barbarea vulgaris (Cabbage family) is the commonest yellow-flowered cress in April and May. It overwinters as a rosette of deeply-lobed, pinnate, dark green leaves, hence the name Wintercress, which refers to its use as a salad herb. The flowering stems are about 25 cm high when flowering begins, and elongate as the lower flowers go to seed, reaching 90 cm. The whole plant is smooth and shiny.

Wintercress is common throughout the British Isles, Europe and northern Asia, especially in damp open roadsides or on river banks. There are three other closely related species which differ in the shape of their stem leaves and in their seed pods. The most distinct is *Barbarea verna* which has pinnate stem leaves with 5–9 pairs of narrow lateral lobes. It is commonest in southern England, being a native of southwest Europe.

Barbarea vulgaris

Primroses

Primrose, Cowslip and Oxlip

Primroses, *Primula vulgaris* (Primrose family), may be a conspicuous sight on north-facing motorway banks and shady hedgerows throughout the British Isles.

Cowslips, *Primula veris*, are rather less common, and favour sunny, drier banks or chalk or limestone areas, again as far north as Sutherland and Orkney. In many areas they have recently become much rarer owing to the ploughing up of so much old pasture, but they can quickly recolonize an area, once it is put down to grass, if they have been able to survive nearby.

Oxlips, *Primula elatior*, are, in the British Isles, confined to old woods in southern East Anglia, but are a conspicuous feature of roadsides in Central Europe, especially along the Autobahns in southern Germany.

Primrose (above); Cowslip (below)

Chickweed

Greater Stitchwort or Satin Flower
Stellaria holostea (Carnation family) is common in hedges and in long grass on roadsides, flowering in April and May. Its stems are thin and floppy, up to 60 cm long, and need grass or bushes for support. The plant is a perennial, often forming large patches, flowering from April to June. The leaves are rough on their margins, and the flowers are 16–25 cm across. Greater Stitchwort is common throughout the British Isles, except for the Scottish Isles.

    Lesser Stitchwort, *S. graminea*, is equally common in grassy places. It has deep green, not bluish, leaves and a smaller flower 5–12 mm across.

    Chickweed, *S. media*, is a universal, annual weed of open ground, and is also found beneath old walls and on roadsides. It is easily recognized by its broad, soft leaves and very small flowers.

Stellaria holostea

Cow Parsley

Cow Parsley, Queen Anne's Lace or Keck

Anthriscus sylvestris (Celery family) is common along roadsides, hedges and on shady banks throughout the British Isles, flowering from April till June. The young leaves emerge in autumn, fresh green with a rather carrot-like smell, which distinguishes them from the soft, faintly aniseed-scented leaves of the **Sweet Cicely**, *Myrrhis odorata*, which is common only in northern England and Scotland. Cow Parsley has smooth fruits 5 mm long, while Sweet Cicely has much larger fruits up to 25 mm.

Other similar later-flowering umbellifers include **Rough Chervil**, *Chaerophyllum temulentum*, which flowers in June and July and is recognized by its purple-spotted and roughly hairy stems, and **Upright Hedge Parsley**, *Torilis japonica*, which flowers a few weeks later, in July and August, and has pinkish or purplish flowers and short, burr-like fruit.

Anthriscus sylvestris

Garlic Mustard

Garlic Mustard, Jack-by-the-Hedge or Hedge Garlic

Alliaria petiolata (Celery family) has small white flowers and flaccid pale green leaves which smell faintly of garlic when crushed. The plant is a biennial, making in the first year a rosette of large, heart-shaped leaves, ready to flower early the following spring from April to June to a height of 120 cm. The whitened, dead stems and remains of the seed pods are conspicuous well into the autumn. Garlic Mustard is common on shady roadsides, in hedges and waste places under trees throughout the British Isles. It is also found throughout Europe, in Asia, including the Himalayas, and in North America.

Alliaria petiolata

Oxford Ragwort

Oxford Ragwort, Squalid Senecio or Inelegant Ragwort

The story surrounding the introduction and spread of *Senecio squalidus* (Daisy family) throughout the British Isles is worth re-telling. It is a native of rocky slopes and gullies in the mountains of southeast Europe, from Italy and Germany to Greece, and from there was introduced to Oxford Botanic Gardens sometime in the early 18th century. Soon it escaped, and by 1890 was well known on almost every wall in and around Oxford. From Oxford it spread all over the country, the parachute-like seeds being sucked along the railway lines which were then being built, and by 1900 it was widespread across England and around Cork. Today it is equally common along roadsides, and in all sorts of open waste places, especially in cities, and after the war it was a characteristic feature of bomb sites. It can be found in flower at almost any time of the year.

Senecio squalidus

Germander Speedwell

Germander Speedwell

Veronica chamaedrys (Figwort family) is the largest flowered and showiest of the native British speedwells, and is common on grassy roadside banks, usually in full sun, throughout the British Isles. It is also found in Europe and northern Asia. The plant spreads by producing creeping stems and can form quite large patches, with stems up to 40 cm high. It flowers from April to June, but may produce a hairy, rounded gall instead of an inflorescence.

On the Continent the larger but similar *V. austriaca* is common. It can be distinguished by its lobed upper leaves. Hoverflies and bees are frequent pollinators. They land on the outstretched stamens which bend under their weight causing the style to come in contact with the underside of the insect. At the same time more pollen is dusted onto the insect's belly.

Veronica chamaedrys

Stork's bill

Common Stork's Bill

Erodium cicutarium (Geranium family) is a common annual by roadsides and in waste places especially on sandy soil and near the sea. The flowers and long beak-like seed pods are rather like a Cranesbill *Geranium* (page 24–29) but the leaves are pinnate with divided feathery leaflets in Stork's Bill, deeply lobed but round in outline in Cranesbills. The whole plant is covered with hairs and sometimes with glands, and may reach 60 cm high. Common Stork's Bill is found wild throughout the British Isles, across Europe and Asia to the Pacific, and is naturalized in North and South America.

Related species are much rarer and usually found on dunes or in short turf. The largest is **Musk Stork's Bill**, *E. moschatum*, which is densely glandular and aromatic, with less divided leaves and obtuse bracts and stipules. It is found on the west coast of England and in Ireland.

Erodium cicutarium

Ox-eye Daisy

Ox-eye Daisy, Moon Daisy, Dog Daisy or Marguerite

Chrysanthemum leucanthemum (Daisy family) is a common perennial on grassy roadsides and in meadows which have not been recently ploughed. It spreads very quickly by seed and often grows in large patches. The dark green leaves are sparsely hairy; the stems tough, with narrow grooves, and are about 40 cm tall. Ox-eye daisies are a familiar sight from late May to June, with a few flowers remaining in August. They are found throughout the British Isles, but are commonest in the south and occur throughout Europe and across northern Asia. The plant is variable in height and flower size, and the most striking forms are dwarf, large-flowered plants growing on cliff tops such as Kynance Cove in Cornwall.

Chrysanthemum leucanthemum

Pyrenaean Cranesbill

Pyrenaean or Mountain Cranesbill

Geranium pyrenaicum (Geranium family) is probably not native in the British Isles, although it was first recorded growing wild as long ago as 1762. Nowadays it is frequently seen along roadsides and railway lines, or in other disturbed grassy places, and is known throughout southern and eastern England, though more rarely in Scotland and Ireland. It is a perennial, with small, purple, deeply bi-lobed petals flowering mainly in June. The whole plant is covered with glandular hairs and grows from 25–50 cm high.

Another species of grassy roadsides, especially on chalk and limestone, is **Long-stalked Cranesbill**, *G. columbinum*. Its smaller, more pinkish-purple flowers have unlobed, usually rounded, petals.

As a native species, Pyrenaean Cranesbill is found mainly in the mountains of Europe, from France to Spain and Portugal, Greece and North Africa.

Geranium pyrenaicum

Cut-leaved Cranesbill

Cut-leaved Cranesbill

Geranium dissectum (Geranium family) is a common annual along roadsides and in waste places throughout the British Isles. Its flowers, which appear in June, are small, with petals about 5 mm long, reddish-pink and lobed at the apex. The stems are spreading, up to 50 cm long, branched, and covered with reflexed hairs. The leaves are hairy beneath, deeply segmented, with narrow pointed lobes. On the Continent Cut-leaved Cranesbill is found throughout Europe, across Asia, and as an alien in North America.

Other similar annual small-flowered Cranesbills such as **Dove's-foot** (see *Weeds* page 63), have less deeply dissected leaves with broader, blunter lobes, and may also be found by roads and in other waste places. **Round-leaved Cranesbill**, *G. rotundifolium*, has pink flowers with rounded petals. It is commonest in southern England, especially in stony and bushy places.

26

Geranium dissectum

Meadow Cranesbill

Meadow Cranesbill

Geranium pratense (Geranium family) is the largest flowered and most conspicuous of the roadside Cranesbills. The flowers are bluish-violet, usually with almost overlapping petals, and very different from **Wood Cranesbill**, *G. sylvaticum*, which has smaller, pinkish or violet flowers, and which is also common in the north of England and Scotland. Meadow Cranesbill is a perennial which can form a clump of long-stalked leaves and a succession of flowering stems up to 80 cm long from June to September. It is common in England but rarer in Scotland and very rare in Ireland, probably native only in Co. Antrim. Other records in Ireland are probably garden escapes; this, and a white-flowered form, are commonly grown in gardens throughout the British Isles.

Geranium pratense

Crosswort

Crosswort and Hedge Bedstraw

Crosswort, *Galium cruciata* (Madder family), is a clump-forming perennial up to 70 cm tall, found growing on sunny banks, amongst scrub, or in rough pasture. The flowers which open in May and June are in about eight flowered cymes; the lateral only male, the terminal hermaphrodite. Crosswort is found throughout the British Isles but is very rare in Ireland.

Hedge Bedstraw, *Galium mollugo* (Madder family), is found in hedges, grassy roadsides and in scrub, especially on calcareous soils throughout the British Isles. Long, branched panicles of white flowers are characteristic, on robust stems up to 120 cm long. Two subspecies are recognized, subsp. *mollugo* with long, straggling stems and flowers 3 mm across in spreading panicles, and subsp. *erectum* with more upright stems and flowers 4 mm across in narrow panicles.

Hedge Bedstraw, *Galium mollugo*

Scentless Mayweed

Scentless Mayweed and Wild Chamomile

Tripleurospermum maritimum subsp. *inodorum* (Daisy family) is the commonest, annual, white-flowered daisy by roadsides and in waste places. Subspecies *maritimum* is an often prostrate perennial, common along the strand line and in other places near the sea. Its glabrous leaves are divided into very narrow segments and are almost scentless when crushed. The flower heads are conical when mature and there are no scales between the disc florets, which are attached to a solid, not hollow receptacle. The very similar Wild Chamomile, *Chamomilla recutita*, is aromatic, has a hollow receptacle and involucral bracts with greenish not brown margins. Other white Chamomile-like daisies have scales between the disc florets.

Scentless Mayweed can be found in flower from July into the autumn and is usually 20–50 cm high. It is common throughout the British Isles and Europe.

Wild Chamomile, *Matricaria recutita*

Ribwort

Ribwort or Black Plantain

Plantago lanceolata (Plantain family) is very common in grassy places and on waste ground. It flowers from April onwards and often again in autumn after the roadsides have been cut. The stems are 10–30 cm long, tough, and deeply grooved beneath the flower head; the leaves are narrow and often have long silky hairs at the base and in the middle of the rosette. Other Plantains can be distinguished by their broader leaves and flower heads; long, narrow and green in **Great Plantain**, *P. major*, shorter and white in **Hoary Plantain**, *P. media*.

Ribwort Plantain is found throughout the British Isles, in Europe and across northern Asia. All plantains have small inconspicuous petals, but large showy anthers hanging on slender filaments, which indicates that they are pollinated by the wind. The seeds also become mucilaginous and sticky when wet, which probably assists in their dispersal and helps them pass through birds without being digested.

Plantago lanceolata

Mouse-ear Hawkweed

Mouse-ear Hawkweed

Hieraceum pilosella (Daisy family) is a small, Dandelion-like plant, common on roadside banks and in other well-drained, dry, sunny places. The flowers are rather pale yellow, the outer reddish on the back; the leaves entire, and sparsely clad with long, rather stiff, white hairs. The plant increases by long runners and so may form extensive patches. The flower stems are from 5–30 cm, usually about 10 cm, and appear from May onwards.

Mouse-ear Hawkweed is common in Britain but rarer in Ireland, and found throughout Europe and western Asia. A closely related rarer species, *H. peleteranum*, is found scattered in southern and western England. It has short, densely-leaved runners.

Other lowland Hawkweeds have many-headed stems. Two common escapes from gardens, called **Fox-and-Cubs**, have reddish-brown flowers and taller stems, but rather similar runners.

Hieraceum pilosella

Bladder Campion

Bladder Campion

Silene vulgaris (Carnation family) is frequent on grassy roadsides and other disturbed waste ground throughout the British Isles, but most commonly in the south. It flowers from June to August. The plant is perennial, making several upright stems from 25–90 cm tall, and the leaves and stem are usually hairless. The flowers may be either hermaphrodite, or unisexual. Female flowers are usually smaller than hermaphrodite ones. The flowers are scented, especially at night and attract night-flying moths, as well as bumble bees. The flowers are often infected by the smut fungus, *Ustilago violacea*, and purple spores are produced instead of pollen grains.

On the Continent Bladder Campion is found in Europe, northern Asia and North Africa. The only closely related British species is **Sea Campion**, *Silene maritima*, a trailing plant with weak stems (see *Coastal Wild Flowers*, page 16–17).

Silene vulgaris

Bulbous Buttercup

Bulbous Buttercup

Ranunculus bulbosus (Buttercup family) is a common perennial buttercup in dry, grassy places. It flowers in May and June, and can then be distinguished from other similar species by having reflexed sepals when the flower is open. The stems are 15–40 cm tall, with appressed hairs above. When not flowering, the bulbous base of the plant, strictly a corm or swollen stem base, is characteristic, and the middle lobe of the leaves have short stalks.

The closely related **Creeping Buttercup**, *R. repens*, has basal leaves with a long-stalked central lobe and runners which make a series of new plants. **Meadow Buttercup**, *R. acris*, does not creep, but has basal leaves with an unstalked central lobe. Both these prefer damper ground than Bulbous Buttercups, and neither have reflexed sepals.

Bulbous Buttercup is common throughout the British Isles and in Europe, except in the extreme south.

Ranunculus bulbosus

Red Clover

White Clover and Red Clover

White Clover, *Trifolium repens* (Bean family), is very common and is often planted along grassy roadsides and on motorway banks. The smooth stems creep along the ground; the flowers which appear in June onwards are sweetly scented and usually pollinated by various bees. White Clover is found throughout the British Isles, Europe, northern Asia and North Africa and has been introduced into other parts of the world. A closely related species, *T. occidentale*, is found by the coast in western England and on the Atlantic coast of Europe.

Red Clover, *Trifolium pratense*, is found in much the same places as White Clover. The flowers are usually pinkish-red, appearing from May onwards, and the plant is tufted, with upright branched stems up to 60 cm high. Red Clover is also frequently planted for fodder, hay or silage and the large cultivated forms have been called var. *sativum.*

White Clover

Hoary Cress

Hoary Cress or Thanet Cress

Hoary Cress, *Cardaria draba* (Cabbage family), is a native of the
Mediterranean and western Asia. According to E. J. Salisbury, it was
introduced to Thanet in Kent in 1809 in hay-stuffed mattresses on which
fever-stricken soldiers were brought back to Ramsgate after an ill-fated
expedition to the island of Walcheren in southern Holland. It is now
common over much of southern England and forms large patches, white
and frothy when in flower, on roadsides and waste ground, spreading by
adventitious buds on the roots. It flowers in May and June on stems 30–90
cm high.

Pepperwort, *Lepidium campestre*, (not illustrated) is a rather similar
annual but has unbranched, erect stems up to 60 cm tall, and small flowers
in a dense spike. The whole plant is grey-green with a thick covering of
minute hairs. It flowers from May onwards, and is common in England,
but rare in Scotland and Ireland.

Cardaria draba

Viper's Bugloss

Viper's Bugloss

Echium vulgare (Borage family) is one of the most beautiful of all roadside flowers with simple or branched spikes of blue flowers up to 90 cm tall. It is usually a biennial, overwintering as a rosette of narrow, bristly leaves and flowering from June onwards. The whole plant is covered with stiff hairs which probably discourage animals such as rabbits from eating it, as it is often conspicuous in heavily-grazed places on sandy soils. Viper's Bugloss is commonest in southern England, especially near the sea, but it is found as far north as southern Scotland. On the Continent it is found throughout Europe and into Turkey.

The individual flowers are tubular with four long-exserted stamens and so are adapted to pollination by hovering moths. Hummingbird Hawk-moths are very fond of them, but they are also visited by bees and other insects.

Echium vulgare

Hemlock showing spotted stem and leaf

Hemlock

Conium maculatum (Celery family) has been notorious for its poisonous properties since ancient Greek times when it was given to Socrates as a form of execution. It contains, among other poisons, the alkaloid coniine, which is found in other poisonous members of the celery family, such as Fool's Parsley. Hemlock is easily identified by its large size, up to 2 metres, smooth, dark purple, spotted stems with a grey bloom, and finely divided leaves. It is found throughout the British Isles but has recently become especially frequent along motorways and by gravel workings in the Thames Valley. The plant is usually a biennial, the seeds germinating in autumn and forming a large rosette of leaves, the plant flowering in June and July and setting seed before dying.

On the Continent Hemlock is found throughout Europe, in North Africa and eastwards to Iran and Lake Baykal in Siberia.

Conium maculatum

Hogweed

Hogweed, Cow Parsnip or Keck

Heracleum spondylium (Celery family) is a coarse, stout biennial, with broad leaflets and roughly hairy stems up to 2 metres. The young flowering stems and leaves can be boiled; they are then excellent to eat, and I have found they compare with asparagus in flavour. The plant flowers throughout the summer, from June to October. On a warm day the flowers give off a smell of pigs, and are visited by large numbers of insects for both nectar and pollen. Hogweed is common on roadsides and waste places throughout the British Isles, across Europe and into northern Asia.

The closely related **Giant Hogweed**, *H. mantegazzianum*, is usually found near rivers and can be distinguished by its larger size and red-spotted stems, 2 to 3.5 metres. It is probably also edible, but can cause a rash if it comes into contact with skin which is subsequently exposed to sun.

Heracleum spondylium

Common Spotted Orchid

Bee Orchid and Spotted Orchid

Bee Orchid, *Ophrys apifera* (Orchid family), is the commonest *Ophrys* in the British Isles and may be found in many places on chalk, limestone or sand-dune soils, and often on roadside banks as it favours places which have recently been disturbed. It is found scattered throughout the British Isles but is absent from northern Scotland. Its success is probably due to the fact that it is habitually self-pollinated, whereas the other *Ophrys* species require specialized insects which mistake the orchid flower for a female and attempt to mate with it.

Spotted Orchid, *Dactylorhiza fuchsii*, is the commonest and most conspicuous pinkish or white orchid on roadsides and may form large colonies on motorway banks, especially on chalky soils or clay. Its lip has three lobes and is marked with spots and lines. The closely related Heath Spotted Orchid is smaller with the middle lobe of the lip less pronounced than the lateral lobes; it is found on acid soils usually among heather.

Bee Orchid

Common Mallow

Common Mallow

Malva sylvestris is the common large-flowered mallow on roadsides and in
waste places. The plant is perennial and sparsely hairy, with spreading or
trailing stems up to 90 cm long and conspicuous purplish-pink flowers up
to 4 cm across from June to September. Common Mallow is found
throughout the British Isles though it becomes rare in Scotland.

Other species of mallow have paler flowers. **Musk Mallow**, *M. moschata*,
is also common on grassy roadsides. It has deeply divided, softly hairy
leaves, and pale pink or white flowers as large as Common Mallow. It is
found commonly in England and southeast Ireland, more rarely in Scotland. The dwarf mallows, *M. neglecta* and *M. parviflora*, are both easily
distinguished by their small flowers, less than 2–5 cm in diameter.

Malva sylvestris

Goat's Beard

Jack-go-to-bed-at-Noon or Goat's Beard

Tragopogon pratensis (Daisy family) is like a dandelion on a tall, grassy-leaved stem. It is generally perennial and found in long grass throughout the British Isles, flowering in June and July. As its name suggests, the flowers are usually open only in the morning; the big 'Clocks' are rather browner and fewer-seeded than those of most dandelions.

Three subspecies are found in the British Isles. Subsp. *minor* has florets shorter than the bracts, and flowers which open only in good weather. Subsp. *pratensis* has large, pale yellow florets, about equal to the bracts, and stays open in dull weather. Subsp. *orientalis*, which is rare and only found in the east, has large, golden yellow florets equalling or longer than the bracts.

Salsify, *T. porrifolius*, is often grown as a vegetable for its long roots. It has purple, not yellow, flowers.

Tragopogon pratensis

Creeping Cinquefoil

Silverweed and Creeping Cinquefoil

Silverweed, *Potentilla anserina* (Rose family), is common along roadsides especially in short grass in places which are damp in winter. The flowering stem is often reddish and can reach a height of 15 cm, and the plant also produces long, trailing stolons which both flower and root to make new plants. The leaves are pinnate and vary greatly in their silkiness. Silverweed is found throughout the British Isles, and in most parts of the temperate world. It flowers from June to August.

Creeping Cinquefoil, *Potentilla reptans*, occurs in similar places though often in shadier places such as grassy tracks through woods. The leaves are not silky, and palmate with usually five leaflets. The flowers are slightly darker yellow and are produced on long creeping stems which root at the nodes. It flowers from June to September and is also common throughout Britain, with the exception of Scotland.

Silverweed, *Potentilla anserina*

Meadow Clary

Meadow Clary

Meadow Clary, *Salvia pratensis* (Deadnettle family), is a strikingly beautiful feature of roadsides in France and Italy, though sadly very rare in Britain and found only on chalk or limestone grassland on the North Downs and the Cotswolds. It reaches a height of 100 cm, and flowers from May to July. The whole plant is hairy and the upper part is also aromatic and sticky with glandular hairs. The flowers are normally 15–25 mm long but there may be smaller, female-only flowers 10 mm long.

Wild Clary, *S. horminioides*, is a more common plant found scattered throughout England and southern Ireland, usually in dry, rocky pasture on roadsides or in sandy places by the sea. It has smaller, deep purple flowers, up to 15 mm long, with two white spots at the base of the lower lip; there may also be cleistogamous flowers only 6 mm long. The plant is also glandular, hairy and slightly aromatic.

Salvia pratensis

Lupin

Lupin

Lupinus polyphyllus (Pea family) is often found on motorway banks or on grassy roadsides and may be a feature of railway embankments. It may be an accidental escape from cultivation, or in some places has probably been deliberately planted, as it grows admirably in poor, sandy soil very low in nitrogen. This lupin is a native of western North America where the flowers are usually blue. Other colours, especially yellow, have been produced by crossing with the **Tree Lupin**, *Lupinus arboreus*, which is also sometimes naturalized in England, especially near the sea.

A third species is the blue-flowered *L. nootkatensis*, found often in large numbers on river shingle in Scotland. It is also a native of western North America, and was introduced into Europe in about 1795 as a garden plant.

Lupinus polyphyllus

Campanula patula

Bellflowers

Campanula patula (Bellflower family) is found in many places in England and Wales, but is never common. In some parts of central Europe however, and particularly in southern Scandinavia, it is a common plant on grassy roadsides and in meadows. It is a biennial or perennial, without hairs, but slightly rough. The leaves are rather narrow and the flowers appear from July to September on many-branched long, wiry stems.

Creeping Bellflower, *Campanula rapunculoides*, is a perennial which spreads underground by slender white roots. It may thus become a weed in gardens and persist on roadsides long after it has been thrown out. The basal leaves are heart-shaped, the short-stalked flowers in a single spike-like raceme, sometimes with secondary racemes at the base. Creeping Bellflower is a native of Europe, from France eastward to Turkey and the Caucasus.

Campanula rapunculoides

Torilis japonica

Wild Carrot and Upright Hedge Parsley

Wild Carrot, *Daucus carota* (Celery family), is common throughout the British Isles on roadsides and other grassy places, especially on chalky soils or sandy places near the coast. It is a biennial, flowering in its second year, between June and August. It is easily recognized by the white or pinkish flowers which become cup-shaped with hairy and bristly fruits; the bracts are long, conspicuous and divided or pinnatifid. The cultivated carrot is subspecies *sativus* and differs mainly in producing a fleshy, edible root in the first year.

Upright Hedge Parsley, *Torilis japonica*, is a common, dull pinkish or purplish-white umbellifer which flowers in July. It is a roughly hairy annual, branching from the base, and up to 125 cm high. The bracts are less conspicuous than those of the carrot, the umbels have 5–12 rays and are not deeply cup-shaped in fruit. The fruits are burr-like, 3–4 mm long, with small crooked spines.

Daucus carota

Ragwort

Ragwort

Ragwort, *Senecio jacobaea* (Daisy family), is commonest on sandy or chalky soils, and may be conspicuous on roadsides or in neglected or over-grazed fields where its poisonous nature protects it even from rabbits. It contains alkaloids, such as jacobine, which damage the livers of sheep and cattle. It flowers from June onwards throughout the British Isles and Europe, and has become a serious weed also in North America and New Zealand.

Hoary Ragwort, *S. erucifolius*, is a rarer plant usually found on heavy soil and in long grass. It is a perennial and can form small clumps of tough, wiry stems, flowering in July and August. It differs from common Ragwort in its leaves which are cottony beneath, and have a small, narrow acute terminal lobe. Its flowers are in looser corymbs. Hoary Ragwort is found mainly in southern and eastern England and only in eastern Ireland.

Senecio erucifolius (left); *S. jacobaea* (right) *S. squalidus* (below: see also page 16)

Musk thistle

Spear Thistle and Musk Thistle

Spear Thistle, *Cirsium vulgare* (Daisy family), is the commonest large purple-flowered thistle in the British Isles. It is a biennial, forming in the first year a very spiny rosette of leaves, and flowering from July to October. It is found throughout the British Isles and is often conspicuous beside mountain roads in Scotland. The stem can reach 150 cm and, as well as spines, has cottony hairs in the grooves and on the undersides of the leaves.

Musk Thistle, *Carduus nutans*, is much rarer, being found mainly on chalky soils in southern England. Its flower heads are large, 3–5 cm in diameter, and drooping, usually set singly on a smooth stem, with rich, reddish-purple flowers. Closely related and sometimes hybridizing with Musk Thistle is **Welted Thistle**, *Carduus acanthoides*, with smaller flower heads in a dense cluster of 3 to 5.

Spear thistle, *Cirsium vulgare*

Red Bartsia

Red Bartsia

Odontites verna (Figwort family) is common on grassy roadsides and by tracks, usually on rather heavy soils or in poorly-drained places. It is found throughout the British Isles. Two subspecies are recognized, but intermediates between them are frequent. Subsp. *verna* which is commonest in Scotland and rare in the south, flowers in June and July. The branches ascend at a narrow angle and the bracts are longer than the flowers. Subsp. *serotina* is common in southern England and Ireland and rare or absent in the north, and flowers in July and August. Its branches are at right angles to the stem with upcurved tips and the bracts are shorter than or equal to the flowers. In both, the stems and leaves are softly hairy and the whole plant may be reddish purple. Red Bartsia is an annual and semi-parasitic, needing to attach itself to the roots of other plants such as grasses before it can grow to its full size which may in exceptional cases be 50 cm.

Odontites verna

Melilotus altissima

Melilots

The three common species of *Melilotus* (Pea family) are tall, branched dainty annuals with small flowers in upright spikes.

White Melilot, *M. alba*, is easily recognized by its white flowers. It is common on roadsides and in waste places, especially in southern England. It is not native but was probably introduced either as a fodder crop or as a contaminant in Lucerne seed (p. 76). Because its seeds can remain viable in the soil for 50 years, White Melilot can come up in unexpected places.

The other species have yellow flowers. **Common Melilot**, *M. officinalis*, has pods similar to White Melilot, glabrous, 3–5 mm long, brown when ripe. **Tall Melilot**, *M. altissima*, has its pods pubescent, 5–6 mm long, and black when ripe. A third, rarer species, **Small-flowered Melilot**, *M. indica*, has smaller flowers about 2 mm long, and a small 2–3 mm long pod, olive green when ripe.

Melilotus alba (right); *M. altissima* (left)

Alfalfa

Lucerne or Alfalfa

Medicago sativa (Pea family) is common in grass along roadsides, especially in southern and eastern England. It is easily recognized by its purple flowers and coiled seed pods. It is a perennial up to 90 cm, but usually around 45 cm, high, flowering from June to September.

Lucerne is a native of southeastern Europe and Turkey but has been widely cultivated in England and Ireland and elsewhere as a drought-resistant fodder crop, and commonly persists for many years.

A hybrid Lucerne, *M. x varia*, is found frequently in East Anglia. Its parents are Lucerne and the yellow-flowered Sickle Medick, *M. falcata*, which is a native of the Breckland. This fertile hybrid has flowers of various interesting shades of black, dark green, and purplish yellow, and fruit between the sickle-shaped pods of *M. falcata* and the coiled pods of *M. sativa*.

76

Medicago sativa

Goat's Rue

Goat's Rue or French Lilac

Galega officinalis (Pea family) is a conspicuous vetch up to 150 cm tall, which has escaped from gardens and become common and conspicuous along roadsides especially in southern England. The flowers are usually lilac, but may be white or pinkish, and appear from June to August. It is native of southern Europe from Germany and France to Greece and Turkey. From the rather similar vetches (*Vicia*) it may be distinguished by the absence of tendrils at the end of the leaves which have 4–8 pairs of leaflets.

Another garden escape, *Coronilla varia*, has rather similar pink, purple or white flowers, arrange in 10–20 flowered heads.

Galega officinalis

Bindweed

Bindweed

Convolvulus arvensis (Convolvulus family) is very common on grassy
road-verges and on waste ground, and is especially conspicuous in dry
summers when its pink flowers are open in July and August. The stems
climb over grasses or creep over bare ground, and may reach 75 cm long. It
is also a terribly persistent garden weed, putting down very deep roots
which can grow up easily from a depth of over 50 cm (and have been found
to a depth of 7 metres) and are resistant to most weedkillers. It spreads
both by seeds and by broken pieces of root, and one plant can cover as
much as 30 square metres in a single season. Bindweed is native throughout
the British Isles and is now found in all temperate parts of the world.

Convolvulus arvensis

Larger Bindweed

Larger Bindweed or Bellbine

Calystegia sepium (Convolvulus family) is a rampant climber usually seen growing over roadside hedges. The flowers are usually white, up to 40 cm long, and the stems may reach 3 metres, often plunging into the ground at their ends and rooting.

Two closely related species have been introduced into gardens and are now found wild. *Calystegia pulchra* has slightly larger flowers, bright pink with white longitudinal bands inside; it is a native of Siberia and North America. *Calystegia sylvatica* has even larger flowers up to 75 mm across which sometimes have pale pink stripes on their outside; it is a native of southern Europe.

The wild white-flowered Bindweed is commonest in southern England and Ireland; the pink-flowered introduced subspecies are commoner in Scotland. A pink-flowered subspecies of *C. sepium* subsp. *roseata* is found wild in western Ireland.

Calystegia sepium

Toadflax

Toadflax

Linaria vulgaris (Figwort family) is conspicuous with its handsome racemes of bright yellow flowers which appear from July until autumn. The leaves are bluish green and smooth, the inflorescence may be glandular and reach 80 cm tall. The flowers usually have one spur and are like 'snapdragons' in shape; occasionally, 'peloric' forms are found which have a regular flower with 5 spurs.

Other common species of Toadflax have smaller purple flowers and are often found on roadsides. *L. purpurea*, an escape from gardens, has stems up to 90 cm long, dense racemes of small, deep purple or, rarely, bright pink flowers. *L. repens* is usually shorter and has slightly larger white or pale lilac flowers with darker veins, in shorter, looser racemes.

Linaria vulgaris

Roadside Grasses

These grasses are all found commonly throughout the British Isles, on roadsides, in meadows and in grassy waste places.

Cock's-foot, *Dactylis glomerata*, forms large tufts of coarse leaves, and produces tough stems up to 100 cm tall from May onwards.

Meadow Fox-tail, *Alopecurus pratensis*, has stems creeping somewhat at the base, and flowering stems up to 80 cm tall from April to June. The softly silky 'fox-tail' is round in section, each spikelet with a single bent awn.

Annual Meadow-grass, *Poa annua*, the commonest small grass of disturbed ground, is soft and sprawling; it may be found in flower throughout the year.

Creeping Fescue, *Festuca rubra*, has a creeping rootstock and flowering stems up to 70 cm tall from May to July. The rather large spikelets, 7–14 mm long, with short awns, distinguish the Fescues from the larger species of meadow grass (*Poa*) which have spikelets up to 7 mm long and no awns.

Crested Dog's-tail, *Cynosurus cristatus*, has tufts of fine leaves and flowering stems up to 75 cm from June to August. The 'dog's tail' is flattened in section, with two rows of rather stiff spikelets.

Perennial Rye-grass, *Lolium perenne*, is a perennial with flowering stems up to 50 cm from May to August. The flattened spike with alternate separate spikelets without awns, is easy to recognize. **Italian Rye-grass** is an annual, commonly planted for fodder. It is most easily distinguished by its awned spikelets.

Left to right: Cock's foot; Meadow Fox-tail; Annual Meadow-grass; Creeping Fescue; Crested Dog's tail; Perennial Rye-grass

False Oat grass, *Arrhenatherum elatius*, is very conspicuous with its oat-like flowers and stems up to 120 cm tall. It is a perennial, flowering mainly in June and July.

Common Bent-grass, *Agrostis tenuis*, is a perennial with a very delicate haze of tiny spikelets 2 to 3.5 mm long. It is usually pinkish in colour, and the inflorescence remains open in fruit, not closed as in **Brown Bent** (*A. canina*) and **Fiorin** (*A. stolonifera*).

Yorkshire Fog, *Holcus lanatus*, is a tufted perennial, very softly hairy, with stems up to 60 cm tall. The very similar **Creeping Soft-grass**, *Holcus mollis* is a more slender plant, commonest on acid, sandy soils, with creeping underground stems like Couch, and long awns.

Timothy, *Phleum pratense*, is rather similar to Meadow Foxtail but has stiffer, smaller spikelets around 3 mm long each with 2 short equal awns, in a cylindrical, blunt-topped panicle.

Reflexed Poa, *Puccinellia distans*, is a salt-marsh grass which has become common along heavily-salted roads inland, often forming a pure sward along the edges of the tarmac, or in muddy lay-bys where lorries pull off. The reflexed branches and leaves rolled even when fresh, are characteristic. The stems may be up to 60 cm tall, with 4–6 branches.

Left to right: False Oat; Common Bent; Yorkshire Fog; Timothy; Reflexed Poa

Everlasting Pea

Everlasting Pea

Lathyrus latifolius (Pea family) is commonly seen on railway embankments, roadsides and on waste ground, where it makes a big, untidy plant with stems up to 2 metres long and bright magenta-pink flowers 20 to 30 mm across. It is a native of southern Europe but has been grown in England since 1596 and commonly escapes. Once established, it is very persistent, hence its name. It flowers from June to August.

Narrow-leaved Everlasting Pea, *L. sylvestris*, is less common but is probably native in woods and hedges mainly in the south. Its leaflets are narrower, 7–15 cm long, flowers smaller, 15–17 mm across, and more flesh-pink in colour, and it has calyx teeth shorter than the tube unlike those of *L. latifolius*.

Lathyrus latifolius

Wild Gladiolus

Wild Gladiolus

Gladiolus illyricus (Iris family) is a very rare native of the British Isles, found only in the New Forest in Dorset and Hampshire. On the Continent, however, it is much more common and found down the west coast of France to Portugal and around the Mediterranean.

Two other species are found occasionally as escapes from gardens, *G. byzantinus* and *G. italicus* of which the latter is a common weed in the cornfields of France and most of southern Europe. The three are not easy to tell apart. In *G. italicus* only the anthers are longer than the filaments, and the seeds are not winged. In *G. illyricus* the stem may reach 50 cm and there are usually 3–10 flowers on the spike which is seldom branched. In *G. byzantinus* the stem is usually more than 50 cm and there are generally 10–20 flowers in a spike which is often branched.

Gladiolus illyricus

Hop Trefoil

Hop Trefoil

Trifolium campestre (Pea family) is a small, yellow-flowered clover found throughout the British Isles on grassy roadsides and dryish meadows. It is an annual and may reach 30 cm in height but is usually around 20 cm. The flowers, which appear from June to September, are typically rather pale yellow when fresh, and then turn pale brown and papery as they fade, enclosing the one-seeded pod.

Lesser Yellow Trefoil, *T. dubium*, is distinguished by its smaller flower heads and dark brown dead flowers in which the standards are narrow and folded over the pod (not flat as in Hop Trefoil), so the seed head appears narrower and smoother in outline.

Trifolium campestre

Horseradish

Horseradish

Armoracia rusticana (Cabbage family) is often found on roadsides, especially in the neighbourhood of old cottages. Its deep tap roots make it difficult to eradicate and one plant can live for many years. The clumps of large, soft, shiny dark green leaves are easy to recognize; the small white flowers in large irregular branched inflorescences appear in June but are less often seen. The leaves can reach a height of 50 cm, the flowering stem 125 cm.

Horseradish is not native of the British Isles but was introduced, probably from southeastern Europe, for its very hot-tasting roots, in about 1600. They are eaten raw, finely chopped or grated, and tamed with cream or yoghurt, or can be preserved by being pickled in salt and vinegar.

Armoracia rusticana

Sainfoin

Sainfoin

Onobrychis viciifolia (Pea family) is a beautiful vetch with an elongated head of pink-veined flowers and short, one-seeded, tubercled seed pods. It is probably native only on dry, chalky soils in southern England, but was commonly planted as a fodder crop and is now found along roads and in rough grassy places over much of southern England and Wales. It is apparently absent from Ireland and Scotland. The plant can reach 60 cm in height and flowering is from June to August.

The other common paler pink-flowered vetches in waste places are escapes from gardens. They are **Crown Vetch**, *Coronilla varia*, which has flowers in flat heads, and **Goat's Rue**, *Galega officinalis*, (see page 78), with heads of pink or lilac flowers. Both have long many-seeded pods.

Onobrychis viciifolia

Wild Mignonette

Wild Mignonette

Reseda lutea (Mignonette family) is a biennial or perennial, found on roadsides, in rough grass and along the edges of arable fields, especially on chalky soils. It flowers from June to September. It is common in suitable places in southern England, but rare in the north, Scotland and Ireland. It is also found in southern and central Europe, and around the Mediterranean.

It can be distinguished from **Dyer's Rocket** or **Weld**, *R. luteola*, by its glabrous, divided leaves and branched stems which give the plant a bushy habit. Dyer's Rocket is aptly named as it has tall, narrow spikes of flowers, as if it were shooting up into the air, and was formerly used to provide yellow dye. It grows in rather similar places but usually in barer ground. Neither species are sweetly fragrant as is the garden Mignonette *R. odorata*, a native of southern Europe.

Weld, *Reseda luteola*

Tufted Vetch

Tufted Vetch and Yellow Vetch

Tufted Vetch, *Vicia cracca* (Pea family), is common throughout the British Isles, scrambling over hedges and in rough grass. It flowers in July and August and the elongated racemes of 10–40 blue-purple flowers are characteristic. Other similar species are found in Europe and the commonest, *V. tenuifolia*, has slightly larger bicoloured white and purple flowers. Yellow Vetch, *V. lutea*, is rare in Britain and found mainly near the sea, as far north as southern Scotland. On the Continent it is common in grassy places, especially in the south around the Mediterranean.

Other purple-flowered species found in Britain are **Bush Vetch**, *V. sepium* with 2–6 flower heads of pale, dirty purple flowers, and the much rarer **Wood Vetch**, *V. sylvatica*, which has white flowers with blue or purple veins.

Yellow Vetch, *Vicia lutea*

St John's Wort

St John's Worts

Hypericum perforatum (St John's Wort family) flowers in late summer, from July to September, and is common in grassy places and hedges throughout the British Isles, though rarer in the north. The leaves, if held up to the light, will be seen to have translucent dots. The plant is perennial, making a tuft of a few stems up to 90 cm tall. The stems are round in section but have two raised lines.

Hairy St John's Wort, *Hypericum hirsutum*, is also common in England, Wales and Scotland, but rare in Ireland. It is similar in general appearance but has hairy leaves and stems and pale yellow flowers. Other stiff, upright St John's Worts have square stems and favour rather damp places. **Square-stemmed St John's Wort**, *H. tetrapterum*, has wings on the angles of the stem, and sepals two thirds the length of the petals. *H. maculatum* has square, but not winged, stems, and sepals a third to a quarter the length of the petals.

Hypericum perforatum

Soapwort

Soapwort or Bouncing Bett

Saponaria officinalis (Carnation family) is usually seen in late summer forming large patches of stems up to 60 cm tall on grassy roadsides. The flowers are usually a beautiful pale pink but can be purplish-pink. Double-flowered forms are as common or more common than the single ones. As an escape from gardens, Soapwort may be found throughout the British Isles, as far north as Aberdeen, and in Ireland, but it is possible that it is native in Devon, Cornwall and north Wales where it is found growing by streams. Damp woods and stream-sides are its usual habitat in Europe and Asia. As its name suggests, a soapy solution was made from the plant, and this has recently been used with benefit on ancient, delicate fabrics.

Saponaria officinalis

Vervain

Vervain

Verbena officinalis (Verbena family) is the only member of the huge and mainly tropical Verbena family to be found wild in Britain. It is a roughly hairy perennial, making a clump of stems up to 60 cm tall, and flowering from July to September. It is never very common, or present in much quantity, but is found scattered throughout England, Wales and Ireland, though not recently seen in Scotland. It tends to persist in the same spot for many years. Vervain was valued in the past as a plant for the treatment of nervous disorders, and a bitter tonic was made from an infusion of the plant.

Verbena offinalis

Chicory

Chicory or Wild Succory
Cichorium intybus (Daisy family) is common on dry roadsides and other waste ground, especially in southern England, though found also in Scotland, Wales and Ireland. It was formerly planted as a fodder crop, especially on chalky soils, as its deep tap roots make it very drought resistant. It is still commonly grown in gardens as a vegetable; the shoots or chichons are blanched by being forced indoors in the dark in winter. Chicory is easily recognized by its tough, many-branched stems and large, bright blue flowers which open only in the morning from July to October. The flower stalks are thickened, the upper stem leaves rather small. Wild plants tend to be hairier and have more deeply lobed leaves than the cultivated variety.

Cichorium intybus

Tansy

Tansy

Tanacetum vulgare (Daisy family) is frequent on grassy roadsides and in rough meadows. It is perennial and forms a clump of strong stems up to 100 cm high. The dirty yellow flowers appear in July and August. The plant is only sparsely hairy but is strong-smelling and was grown and used as a medicinal and pot herb. Medicinally it was used to scour the stomach to get rid of worms, especially in very young children, and the young leaves were made into puddings or pancakes and eaten particularly on Easter day. It was also used as a spicy flavouring in milk puddings and cakes, and even in sausages in Ireland. Tansy is possibly native in southern England, but was so commonly cultivated that it is now found throughout the British Isles. It is found also throughout Europe and into western Asia.

Tanacetum vulgare

Evening Primrose

Evening Primrose
Oenothera erythrosepala (Willowherb family) is one of the many different species of Evening Primrose introduced originally as garden plants and now naturalized on roadsides, waste ground and dunes throughout the British Isles and Europe. The original species came from North America but some new species, including *O. erythrosepala* originated in Europe by hybridization and have even become naturalized in America. The plants are biennial, making a flat rosette of leaves in the first year, and a tall, flowering stem in the second, up to 1 metre tall. The flowers, which are sweet-scented, open around sunset and fade in the morning, especially on hot days. Their scent attracts Hawkmoths and noctuids; the pollen is unusual in that it is not powdery, but in strings, attached by minute elastic threads. Recently the seed of Evening Primrose has been found to contain a valuable and nutritious oil, and it is beginning to be cultivated on a field scale.

Oenothera erythrosepala

Greater Knapweed

Knapweed, Hardheads or Blackheads and Greater Knapweed

Centaurea nigra (Daisy family) is common on grassy roadsides and in meadows throughout the British Isles. The plant is perennial and produces tough, roughly hairy stems up to 60 cm tall. The plants are very variable in thickness of stem and in the colour and shape of the appendages to the bracts which cover the base of the flower heads. These appendages are usually triangular, narrowing abrubtly into the bract.

Sometimes Knapweed has the outer florets of the head enlarged. It then resembles Greater Knapweed, *C. scabiosa*, which is found especially on chalk or limestone soils, or on sand dunes. It is found throughout England, Scotland and Ireland but is nowhere as common as *C. nigra*. Greater Knapweed is usually larger and has deeply pinnated basal and stem leaves, and appendages to the bracts which are decurrent and horseshoe-shaped.

Knapweed, *Centaurea nigra*

Lesser Burdock

Lesser Burdock

Arctium minus (Daisy family) is common on grassy roadsides, in hedges and scrub and in open woods throughout the British Isles, especially so on heavy, rich soils or near water. It is a biennial, forming broad, soft, long-stalked basal leaves and a branched inflorescence up to 130 cm high. The thistle-like flowers open in July and have spiny hooked tips, so the whole seed head can become attached to passing animals' fur or clothing, and the seeds dispersed away from the parent plants. Several subspecies have been distinguished but they are very difficult to tell apart.

The closely related **Greater Burdock**, *A. lappa*, has fewer large flower heads and the petiole of the basal leaves is solid, not hollow.

The long tap roots of the young plants are eaten roasted, especially in Japan, where the plants are commonly cultivated. The young shoots can also be eaten boiled.

Arctium minus

Beaked Hawk's-beard

Beaked Hawk's-beard

Crepis vesicaria, subsp. *haensleri* (Daisy family) is a common, usually biennial, plant up to 80 cm tall. It is found on roadsides and in rough grassy places, mainly in southeastern England and in southern Ireland, flowering from May to July. It is native of southern Europe, but has been known in England since the early 18th century.

Rough Hawk's-beard, *Crepis biennis*, is rather similar, but much less common. It flowers rather later, and has slightly larger flower heads with golden-yellow florets, the outer not reddish beneath, and stem leaves without pointed lobes at the base. It is found scattered throughout eastern England and central Ireland.

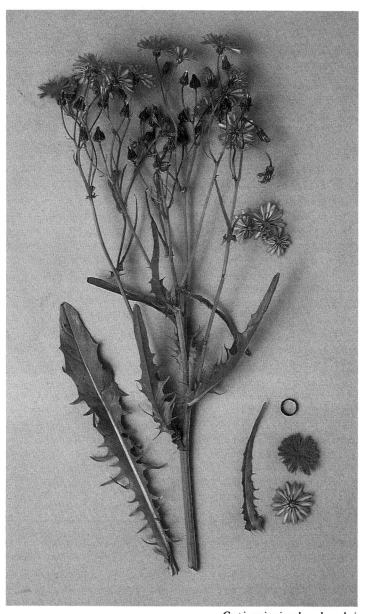

Crepis vesicaria subsp. *haensleri*

Leontodon autumnalis

Smooth Hawks-beard

Crepis capillaris (Daisy family) has branched stems with 1 or 2 well-developed leaves around the base of the main branches. It has rather small flower heads, 1–1.3 cm in diameter when open. The whole plant is often almost hairless and generally delicate in appearance.

Autumnal Hawkbit, *Leontodon autumnalis*, has only scaley leaves on the branched stems which can reach 60 cm. The flower heads are 1.2–3.5 cm in diameter, often woolly on the outside. Both are very common throughout the British Isles.

The situation is complicated by an unusual form of *C. capillaris*, var. *glandulosa*, with larger flower heads, up to 2.5 cm across, covered with dark glandular hairs around their base. A mountain variety of *Leontodon autumnalis*, var. *pratensis*, also has blackish woolly hairs around the base of the flower head which may be solitary.

Crepis capillaris

Field Sow Thistle

Bristly Ox-tongue

Bristly Ox-tongue, *Picris echioides* (Daisy family), is easily recognized by its bristly hairy texture, the stiff hairs on the leaves with pale swollen bases. It often occurs on waste ground in southern and eastern England and is most common on the coast. It is absent from Scotland and, in Ireland, found only near Dublin and Wexford. **Hawkweed Ox-tongue**, *P. hieracioides*, is found in much the same areas. It can be distinguished by being less bristly and by its narrow bracts around the stem of the flower head.

Field Sow-Thistle, *Sonchus arvensis*, is a tall, handsome plant with its large orange-yellow heads and dense glandular hairs around the base of the flower heads. It is found commonly throughout the British Isles by roadsides, in waste places, and on shingle by the sea. It is a perennial, spreading underground by white brittle rhizomes and so can form large patches and become a pest in gardens.

Picris echioides

Prickly Lettuce

Prickly Lettuce

Two species of wild lettuce are common by roadsides and in waste places in southern England, especially in the southeast and around London, but they are uncommon elsewhere, and unknown in Ireland. They are conspicuous in late summer with their tall, stiff stems showing above the dying grass, and their hundreds of small, dandelion-like flowers. The upper leaves are bristly around the edges, and the plants exude a milky juice when broken. The two species, *Lactuca serriola*, and *Lactuca virosa* (Daisy family) are similar in general appearance but *L. virosa* has less divided leaves and black, not grey, ripe fruit. In *L. serriola* the leaves have the unusual feature of being held vertically, not flat as in most plants. Both these species are most common in southern Europe and rare in the north, reaching their northwestern limit in England.

Lactuca serriola

Fleabane

Fleabane

Pulicaria dysenterica (Daisy family) is common in wet ditches and grassy roadsides throughout southern England and Ireland, though rare in northern England and almost absent in Scotland, except in the south around the coast. It is a perennial, forming large patches by means of creeping stems, flowering from July to September. The stems are up to 50 cm high and woolly, as are the undersides of the leaves. As its name suggests it was used against fleas, and medicinally, against dysentry.

Lesser Fleabane, *Pulicaria vulgaris*, is much rarer and found only in a few places in south central England. It is an annual, with much smaller flower heads and erect, short ligules which are not longer than the involucre.

Pulicaria dysenterica

Agrimony

Agrimony

Agrimonia eupatoria (Rose family) is common on grassy roadsides and in meadows throughout most of the British Isles, though rare in northern Scotland. Its small yellow flowers appear in July and August in long narrow spikes up to 50 cm high. In fruit, they become burrs with numerous hooked spines which can be dispersed by animals and on clothing. Each burr contains one or two seeds. The leaves and stems are softly hairy.

A second species, *A. procera*, often known as *A. odorata*, is rarer but found scattered over the same range as *A. eupatoria*. It differs by being tetraploid and in several other minor characters; the petals are often emarginate, some of the spines of the burr are reflexed towards the stem, and the burr itself is somewhat larger. The stem has hairs all of one length, not of different lengths, as is found in *A. eupatoria*.

Agrimonia eupatoria

Yarrow

Yarrow or Millfoil

Achillea millefolium (Daisy family) is common throughout the British Isles in grassland and by roadsides. It is a perennial and exceptionally drought-resistant, in dry summers surviving and flowering when the surrounding grass has become brown. It is very variable in height and may reach 60 cm; the flowers are usually white but may be pink, and open from June onwards. The flowers are crowded into a flat-topped inflorescence. The leaves are softly hairy and aromatic, and were used to treat wounds.

Sneezewort, *Achillea ptarmica*, has fewer, larger flowers, and narrow, toothed, undivided leaves. It is usually found in damp soil, in ditches or in marshes, and is most common in the north and west of the British Isles.

Achillea millefolium

Black Horehound

Black Horehound and White Horehound

Ballota nigra, the Black Horehound (Deadnettle family), is common in roadside hedges flowering from June to October. It is found most commonly in the south and east of England and is absent from the mountains, from most of Scotland and Ireland where it is known only as an introduction, probably as a medicinal herb. The stems may reach 100 cm and the whole plant has a strong and disagreeable smell.

White Horehound, *Marrubium vulgare*, is much less common being possibly native along the south coast of England and Wales and otherwise scattered throughout the British Isles, as an escape from cultivation. It differs from Black Horehound in its white flowers and rounded leaves. It has ten long teeth on the calyx, whereas Black Horehound has five. **Catmint**, *Nepeta cataria*, is rare on roadsides and in hedges, and is usually found on chalk. It has white flowers in loose heads, and the calyx has five teeth.

White Horehound, *Marrubium vulgare*

White Mullein, *V. lychnitis*

Mullein or Aaron's Rod

Verbascum thapsus (Figwort family) is the most common of several Mulleins in the British Isles and easily recognised by its grey woolly stems
which can reach 2 metres, and soft, felt-like leaves. It is found throughout
the British Isles in dry waste places, but is rarest in western Scotland and
the Highlands. The plant is a biennial forming in the first year a rosette of
large stemless leaves, and flowering the following June.

Other Mulleins found by roadsides have smaller flowers and more
delicate spikes. **Dark Mullein**, *V. nigrum*, is found most commonly on the
chalk from East Anglia to Wiltshire and in south Cornwall. It has dark
green leaves which are not woolly on the surface, and yellow flowers with
striking purple hairs on the anther filaments. **White Mullein**, *V. lychnitis*,
is commonest in Kent and has branched spikes of small, usually white,
flowers.

Verbascum thapsus

Teasel

Teasel

Dipsacus fullonum (Teasel family) is tall and conspicuous on damp road-sides near rivers or on heavy soil. The pale purple, thistle-like flower heads and the opposite pairs of stem leaves, the lower of which are fused to form a cup around the stem, make it easy to recognize. The cup may often hold dew or rainwater as well as various dead insects and other debris. The Teasel is a biennial, forming a rosette of crisp, bristly leaves in the first year, and putting up branched flowering stems to a height of 2 metres the following July. It is commonest in southeastern and central England, mainly coastal in Wales and Ireland, and found only in the southeast of Scotland.

Wild Teasel has straight spines on the flower head. **Fuller's Teasel,** *D. sativus,* has hooked spines and was formerly cultivated for carding wool. It is now very rare.

Dipsacus fullonum

Wild Parsnip

Wild Parsnip

Pastinacia sativa (Celery family) is very common in southeast England and south Wales but rare in Ireland and north and west of the Humber and Severn. It is the most common yellow-flowered umbellifer on roadsides, reaching a height of 150 cm, and flowering from June to August. The plant is a biennial, in the first year producing coarse, pinnate basal leaves, and flowering and fruiting in the second year. This is the species from which the cultivated parsnip is derived, by selecting plants with a thickened tap root at the end of the first year.

The only other common yellow-flowered umbellifer is the **Fennel**, easily distinguished by its leaves which are finely divided into hair-like segments. It is found mainly near the coast in England, Wales and Ireland.

Pastinaca sativa

Pimpinella major

Burnet Saxifrage and Greater Burnet Saxifrage

Pimpinella saxifraga (Celery family) is common in dry grassland and on roadsides throughout the British Isles, though rare in northern Ireland and northwest Scotland. The Burnet Saxifrage has a tough and hairy branched stem and can reach 100 cm, but it is usually around 40 cm high, and its white flowers are open in July and August. Its leaves can vary greatly in shape but are usually two-pinnate with ovate to linear-lanceolate segments.

Pimpinella major, the Greater Burnet Saxifrage, is rarer, though common in a few areas such as Kent, the Midlands and Lincolnshire, in south Devon and around Limerick. It differs mainly in its angled, hollow stem which is smooth and brittle, and in its fruit with whitish ridges. It prefers damper places, hedgerows or the edges of woods, and flowers earlier in June and July.

Pimpinella saxifraga

Russian Vine

Russian Vine

Bilderdykia aubertii (Bistort family) is commonly sold as a fast climber to cover concrete garages, sheds and other eye-sores in as short a time as possible. It has often exceeded its intended use, and can be seen covering hedges, and climbing up trees, to a height of 20 metres, beautiful in late summer with cascades of white flowers and pink hanging fruit. The plant has a perennial rootstock and the shoots can also become shrubby and remain over winter. It is a native of western China and Tibet, introduced in 1899. Closely related but rarer is the pink-flowered *B. baldschuanica*, a native of Tadzhikistan in central Asia. It also differs in having an almost smooth axis to the inflorescence.

Bilderdykia aubertii

Japanese Knotweed

Japanese Knotweed

Reynoutria japonica (Bistort family), often called *Polygonum cuspidatum*, is a giant rampant perennial, which forms a forest of hollow stems up to 2 metres high. It was introduced from Japan to grow in the wild gardens then fashionable, but soon outgrew its welcome and was thrown out, often onto the roadside where it continued to flourish. The pointed shoots appear in spring, the branched panicles of white flowers in the leaf axils in August, lasting till October. It is found throughout the British Isles, most commonly around London, and on the west coast.

The very similar *R. sachalinensis* is rarer; it is even larger, with greenish flowers and leaves more than 15 cm long, somewhat heart-shaped at the base.

Reynoutria japonica

Old Man's Beard

Traveller's Joy or Old Man's Beard

Clematis vitalba (Buttercup family) is common, growing over hedges in southern England and Wales. It is also found in Ireland, but is probably not native there, nor in Scotland where it is found in only a few places. It is surprising that a plant, so common on chalk and limestone in southern England, should be so rare in the north where soils would seem suitable. It is possible that summer temperatures are too low in the area north of the Humber. Furthermore, it is not native in Denmark, Sweden and Norway, but is common over most of the rest of Europe. The climbing stems, which become woody, can reach 30 metres when climbing up trees; the flowers which are sweet-scented are open in July and August and are followed by fruits with curled, silky styles which last into the winter.

Clematis vitalba

Hop bine

Hop
Humulus lupulus (Hemp family) is a perennial which puts up long, rough climbing shoots every year, up to 6 metres high. They are common, scrambling over hedges; they flower in July and August, fruiting from August onwards. Male and female flowers grow on separate plants. The male flowers are small and consist of a mass of stamens. The female fruiting heads, which look like small, elongated Brussel Sprouts, are richly aromatic and it is these that are used to flavour beer to make it bitter. For this reason the plant has been much cultivated and is now found throughout the British Isles though it is probably truly native only in England and Wales; it is fairly frequent in Ireland and rare in Scotland.

Humulus lupulus

White Bryony

White Bryony

Bryonia cretica (Cucumber family) is the only member of this family native in the British Isles. From a huge, tough rootstock, annual climbing stems can reach 4 metres in the season, attaching themselves to hedges and shrubs by coiling tendrils. The male and female flowers are rather similar but are produced on separate plants. The ripe fruits are red. White Bryony is common in southeastern England but rare in Wales and the southwest, and reaching only as far north as Yorkshire in the east. It is not found in Ireland or Scotland.

Black Bryony, *Tamus communis*, is superficially rather similar but has very shiny green leaves and no tendrils but climbs with its coiling stems. Its minute green flowers are in long spikes. It flowers from June to September.

Bryonia cretica

Spear-leaved Orache

Spear-leaved Orache

Atriplex prostrata (syn *hastata*) (Goosefoot family) has recently become a conspicuous feature of the edges of roads in many parts of England. Over most of the British Isles it is a coastal species and because it is tolerant of salt, it grows well along roads which are heavily salted in winter, often forming a band a metre or so wide between the tarmac and the grass. Other coastal species have recently spread inland along these salty verges, notably the **Salt-marsh Grass**, *Puccinellia distans*, and the **Sea Plantain**, *Plantago maritima* (see *Coastal Wild Flowers*, pages 74 and 132). The species of Orache can be recognized by their large triangular fruits. The commonest *Chenopodium*, **White Goosefoot**, *C. album*, with mealy leaves and numerous much smaller fruits, is found on roadsides as well as in other waste places. Spear-leaved Orache has distinctly arrowhead-shaped leaves which distinguish it from the commoner *A. patula* which has lanceolate or linear upper leaves.